André
Bessette

A Heart of Strength

1845–1937
Born in Mont-Saint Grégoire,
near Montreal, Quebec, Canada
Feast Day: January 6
Patronage: People who are sick
or handicapped, and poor people

Text by Barbara Yoffie
Illustrated by Katherine A. Borgatti

Liguori
ONE LIGUORI DRIVE
LIGUORI MO 63057-9999

Dedication

To my family:
my parents Jim and Peg,
my husband Bill,
our son Sam and daughter-in-law Erin,
and our precious grandchildren
Ben, Lucas, and Andrew

To all the children I have had the privilege of
teaching throughout the years.

Imprimi Potest:
Harry Grile, CSsR, Provincial
Denver Province, The Redemptorists

Published by Liguori Publications
Liguori, Missouri 63057

To order, call 800-325-9521
www.liguori.org

p ISBN 978-0-7648-2240-7
e ISBN 978-0-7648-6800-9

Liguori Publications, a nonprofit corporation, is an apostolate of The
Redemptorists. To learn more about The Redemptorists, visit Redemptorists.com.

Printed in the United States of America
17 16 15 14 13 / 5 4 3 2 1
First Edition

Dear Parents and Teachers:

Saints and Me! is a series of children's books about saints. Six books make up the first set: *Saints of North America.* In this set, each book tells a thought-provoking story about a heavenly hero.

Saints of North America includes the heroic lives of six saints from the United States, Canada, and Mexico. Saints Kateri Tekakwitha and Elizabeth Ann Seton were both born in the United States. Saint Juan Diego was born in Mexico, and Saint André Bessette was from Canada. European missionaries also came to North America to spread the Catholic faith, making it their home while they worked with people in the New World. Saints Rose Philippine Duchesne and Damien de Veuster were missionary saints.

Through the centuries, saints have always been dear to Catholics, but *why*? In most instances, ordinary people were and are transformed by the life of Jesus and therefore model Christ's life for us. It is our Lord who makes ordinary people extraordinary. As your children come to know the saints, it is our hope that they will come to understand and identify that they, too, are *called to be saints.*

Which saint wanted to work with Native Americans? Who wanted to work with the sick people on the island of Molokai, Hawaii? To which saint did the Virgin Mary appear? Who loved Saint Joseph? Which saint started the first American religious community of women? Do you know which saint is the patron of nature? Find the answers in the *Saints of North America*, *Saints and Me!* set and help your child identify with the lives of the saints.

Introduce your children or students to the *Saints and Me!* series as they:

—**READ** about the lives of the saints and are inspired by their stories.

—**PRAY** to the saints for their intercession.

—**CELEBRATE** the saints and relate to their lives.

saints of north america

 Kateri Tekakwitha

 Juan Diego

 Rose Philippine Duchesne

 Damien of Molokai

 Elizabeth Ann Seton

 André Bessette

Belgium

France

Alfred Bessette was born in a small town near Montreal, Canada. When Alfred was a baby he was often sick. His mother would hold him and whisper, "Little Alfred, you will get better soon."

The Bessette family did not have a lot of money, but they had faith in God. Prayer was very important to them. When Alfred prayed, he felt very close to God. He felt peaceful and happy.

Alfred was nine years old when his father died in an accident. A few years later his mother died of tuberculosis.
Now orphans, the Bessette children went to live with relatives.

Alfred went to live on a farm with his aunt and uncle. He tried to do his chores. "Can you feed the chickens for me?" asked his uncle. The bucket of feed was heavy. Alfred had trouble lifting it.

"There must be a job I can do,"
thought Alfred. Over the next few years
he worked as a baker, a shoemaker, and
a factory worker. The work was too hard.
Alfred got sick.

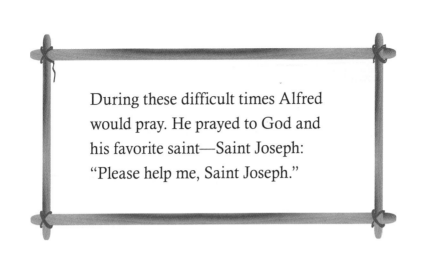

During these difficult times Alfred would pray. He prayed to God and his favorite saint—Saint Joseph: "Please help me, Saint Joseph."

Father André Provençal was a parish priest. He knew Alfred. He talked to Alfred about God and Saint Joseph. They talked about vocations, too. "Maybe God is calling you," the priest said. "But I am not very strong and not very smart," Alfred answered. "Don't worry. Just pray," said Father Provençal.

And that is just what Alfred did.
He prayed and asked Saint Joseph
to help him. At age twenty-five he joined
the Congregation of Holy Cross
as a brother.

Alfred was now called Brother André.
He worked very hard. Brother André
grew closer to God each day.
Soon he made lots of friends
and was very happy.

His first job there was as a doorkeeper
at Notre Dame College in Montreal.
He was so excited! Brother André
would greet everyone who came to visit.
"Welcome, come in! Can I help you?"
There was always a smile on his face.

Sometimes people would tell him
sad stories. Other times the stories
were about sickness or pain.
Brother André would always tell them,
"I will pray for you.
I will pray to
Saint Joseph."
The people would
thank him and smile.
He made them
feel good.

People would come back to Brother André
to tell him they had been cured.
"It is a miracle! I am healed!" Brother
André would reply, "God makes miracles
happen. I prayed to Saint Joseph for you.
I did not heal you."

There were many more stories of miracle healings. Thousands of people, young and old, told of cures from Brother André's prayers. He became known around the world for his gift of healing. Crowds of people came to visit him and ask for his prayers.

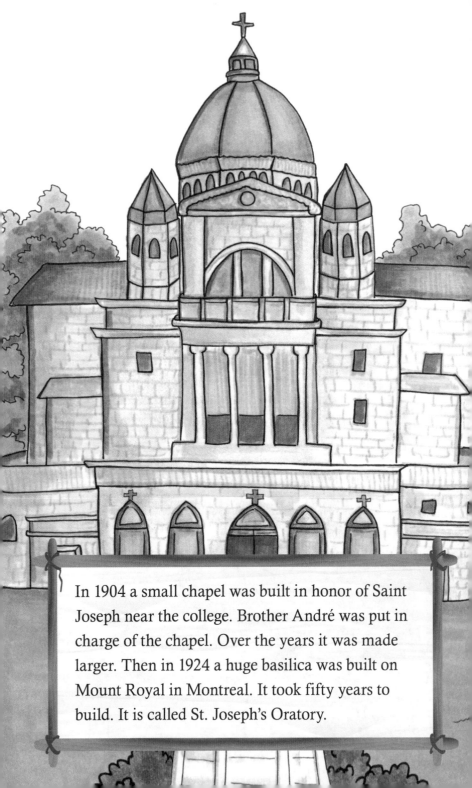

In 1904 a small chapel was built in honor of Saint Joseph near the college. Brother André was put in charge of the chapel. Over the years it was made larger. Then in 1924 a huge basilica was built on Mount Royal in Montreal. It took fifty years to build. It is called St. Joseph's Oratory.

Brother André died in 1937. He is buried
in this beautiful church. It was his dream
to have a church built in honor of Saint Joseph.
The Oratory is visited by more than two
million pilgrims each year.

Saint André Bessette is called the
"Miracle Man of Montreal."
His heart was filled
with faith, love,
and strength.

*A miracle is
just God's way
to show
he loves us
every day.*

Dear God.

I love you.

Saint André

loved you, too.

He also

loved Saint Joseph.

Fill my heart

with faith and love.

Give me strength

when I need help.

Amen.

NEW WORDS (Glossary)

Basilica: A special and very large church

Brother: A member of a religious order who takes special vows

Chapel: A small church

Congregation of Holy Cross: A religious order founded by Blessed Basil Moreau in 1837

Miracle: A wonderful event that cannot be explained. A miracle shows God's love for us.

Oratory: A place of prayer and worship

Orphan: A child whose parents have died

Pilgrim: A person who travels to a holy place to pray

Tuberculosis: A serious illness that affects the lungs

Vocation: A call from God to serve him in a special way

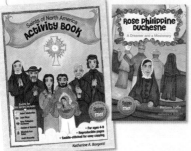